THE NEED FOR A BRIDGE

poems by

Joyce Wilson

Finishing Line Press
Georgetown, Kentucky

THE NEED FOR A BRIDGE

Copyright © 2019 by Joyce Wilson
ISBN 978-1-63534-857-6 First Edition
All rights reserved under International and Pan-American Copyright Conventions. No part of this book may be reproduced in any manner whatsoever without written permission from the publisher, except in the case of brief quotations embodied in critical articles and reviews.

ACKNOWLEDGMENTS

The following poems, some in different form under different titles, appeared in the following publications:

"The Birdwatcher" in *American Arts Quarterly*
"The Journalist" in *Grey Sparrow*
"The Dreamer" in *Ibbetson Street*
"The Engineer" and "The Foreman" in *Main Street Rag*
"The Provider," "The Captain," "The Naturalist" in *Muddy River Poetry Review*
"The Ferry," "The Commuter," "The Librarian," "The Player," "The Celebrant," on *The Poetry Porch*

Publisher: Leah Maines
Editor: Christen Kincaid
Cover illustration: *1936 Art Deco Bridge over the Fore River* by Allegra Printz
Author Photo: John Goldie
Cover Design: Leah Huete

Printed in the USA on acid-free paper.
Order online: www.finishinglinepress.com
 also available on amazon.com

Author inquiries and mail orders:
Finishing Line Press
P. O. Box 1626
Georgetown, Kentucky 40324
U. S. A.

Table of Contents

The Ferry: Up to 1800 1

The Commuter: Frustration in Contemporary Times 2

The Journalist: A New Bridge Unlikely 3

The Engineer: Bascule, Swing, or Lift 4

The Optimist: 1925 5

The Foreman: Landmark Down, 1934 7

The Librarian: A Brief History 8

The Birdwatcher: Signs of Disorder 9

The Dreamer: Suspended on the Bridge 10

The Lurker: Underneath the Bridge 11

The Player: His Crossing Pass 12

The Salesman: The Gantry Crane 13

The Pilot: Laws and Regulations 14

The Operator: Facts 15

The Provider: This Bridge Will Get You 16

The Baker: Time to Rise 17

The Captain: Of the Seas 19

The Minister: In Memoriam 20

The Naturalist: River Gods 21

The Celebrant: We Look Out Over the Water 22

Notes 25

To the Thomas Crane Public Library of Quincy, Massachusetts, whose collections foster the pursuit of history and research.

The Ferry: Up to 1800

Seventy-year-old Miss Sally Fulton
Was waiting for the ferry on her way
From Quincy to Hingham, where land was split
By rivers, one called Fore, the other Back.

She could have circled back, around, and north
Up Payne's Hill through Braintree on winding roads;
Instead she headed south, a line direct
To Ferry Point, low on the Quincy side.

She watched the tiny flatbed ferry floating
Toward her over murky river waves,
Her horse uneasy as the phaeton leaned
Against the slope of gravel underfoot.

Once they had lurched onto the rocking deck,
The nervous look of her gray mare, white-eyed,
And sudden rustling sounds loosed from her skirts,
Their snap against the gusts portending rain,

Might have spoken to her just then as signs
Of changing tides and the need for a bridge.

The Commuter: Frustration in Contemporary Times

The guard-lights blink, the bar comes down. A boy
Dragging his feet would best describe the speed
Of iron grillwork flooring inching up,
Its patterns rippling in reflective light.

Progress has become hurry up and wait,
One length forward, and then the siren warns;
At rest, or stuck, we watch the tanker pass
Below, our patience tested by its fate.

We cannot cross until the laden ship
Has cleared the measured span. We curse our luck.
The upraised flooring shudders like a sail
That will not take its sailors anywhere.

The Journalist: A New Bridge Unlikely

Who: Fore River Bridge
What: must be replaced
Where: between Quincy and Weymouth, Massachusetts
When: in the near future

The iron swing bridge of 1902
Had been replaced in 1936
By a double-draw of ornamented style
With Art Deco handrails in bronze detail.

The bascule bridge caused several accidents
That added to the traffic and complaints;
Soon pleas for a new structure reached the state:
Send us a bridge to love, not love to hate.

The temporary, all that we could get,
Soon earned its given name, Erector Set;
With panels, pins, and bolts on shaky piers,
They built the thing to last for fifteen years.

Not one to be the bearer of bad news,
I call this bridge a comedy of errors.

The Engineer: Swing, Bascule, Lift

The swing design pivoted the road
Itself to let the river traffic through,
Like a spigot cutting water flow
With right angles to stop, aligned to go.

Bascule combines the Old French word for low
Or bas, with Latin for backside, or cul,
In which one end mimics sitting down
While the other raises up its arm.

Like the drawbridge over algaed motes
That separated castles from the hordes,
Bascule revives an ancient rivalry
Where former friends divide in enmity,

Which might explain what set its plan adrift
In preference for that of vertical lift.

The Optimist: 1925

The Optimist, a South Shore Wayfarer
Calls fog dense and amiable, a swaddler

Of vanished ground, wrapping all he sees
In a belief of progress he describes;

Is sympathetic with the motor sounds,
the puff puff of the energetic tug

That leans its shoulders to the weighty barge
And pushes it, through the opened bridge;

Calls the vermilion patchwork under-painting
Of the wharf "immaculate" with dust,

Coal dust from factory stacks of the plant
Seen in the distance, tall, slender, and proud;

Deems ark-like skeletons of the drydocks
Less vital than the energy on water;

Concludes that the electric plant, splendid
In its novelty, must work to mask

Its role as an intruder, though bold
In its demeanor, new to the block;

Sees in the future, once the fog lifts, a glimpse
Of the same picture, with more smokestacks and boats

That bring more growth and geniality
To these environs, Nineteen Twenty-five;

And stands up tall to make his vision spin,
To dive and duck and take it on the chin

As he might bluff and bluster to project
The quality of life that we expect.

He does not face what he cannot control:
The depths below, the fear that he might fall,

The signs of trouble underneath the wall,
Polution, waste, no warnings there at all.

The Foreman: Landmark Down, 1934

The ground ripped open, and the quiet gone,
This bridge-work occupies connecting towns.
The elms that once provided ample shade
Across the streets and lawns have all come down.

Colonial homes razed by the wrecker's tools
Are hauled and crunched and stacked in lumber yards.
First hollow sounds of the workman's rhythmic axe,
Then trucks that roar and snort like hungry dogs.

Now steam shovels, a new breed of machine,
Have taken out the 1800 bridge.
A landmark for ten thousand dollars then
Will cost more than two million dollars now.

And who will say the cost will be too much,
And who will do the work to prove its worth?

The Librarian: A Brief History
    Through Headlines from The Patriot Ledger

The first was nothing but a timber pile.
In Eighteen Twelve, they tried the swing design.
The story of the boulder on the scow
That threw the draw one summer day, July,
Nineteen Eighteen, when boat and rock were fixed
Beneath the bridge until the tides went out,
Foretold the brand new floor of 'Twenty-five;
But then, in 'Thirty-four, that bridge was down,
Razed and replaced with the bascule design,
Which failed to open in 'Thirty-Seven
And failed to close in Nineteen Fifty-one.
The draw-tenders were asked to help out in
The curbing of spying, Nineteen Thirty-nine,
And a home-made bomb removed in 'Sixty-eight.
The birds who came in Nineteen Seventy
Were urged to leave with a recorded cry,
Then poisoned by the DPW.
The lone woman who leaped from the railing
Did not die in Nineteen Seventy-four
Because she landed in forgiving sand,
But the boy driving through the heavy rains
Did die, and his father blamed the bridge, with signs
Protesting that the surface weave could kill.
Now the flexible bascule bridge has been
Condemned, in Nineteen Eighty-six, and paired
With an experimental lift design
Until the towns decide what kind they want.
Now in the town report, the space beneath
The heading "aesthetics" has been left blank.

The Birdwatcher: Signs of Disorder

Isolated near the sea, the bridge
Engages them, and all along its struts,
They settle overnight, shoulder to shoulder.

At dawn, they rise from points like filings flung
Against some scrim of fabric in the sky
And drawn by unseen magnets into shapes.

The birds shake out the shadows of their wings
And darken all the edges of the bridge
Like manic artists who'd correct its form.

We hear their cries above the traffic's din
And fear that hidden in their minds' dark color
We might detect some permanent disorder.

The Dreamer: Suspended on the Bridge

The driver gets out of his car to watch
The bridgegates in their mechanized ascent.
He leans over the metal rail to match
His mood with twilight's quiet argument,

And then the motors' low murmuring idle
And shush of waves against the tugboat's shoulder
Surprise him with the music of their babble.
He wants their tranquil sounds to last forever.

The moment bursts, infectious like a fever.
An idler's dreaming must give way to motion.
Beneath the rhythmic noises of the harbor,
The tide releases currents to the ocean.

As engines roll, each lane in single file,
He takes a breath and cannot help but smile.

The Lurker: Underneath the Bridge

Consistent with his reputation as
A shirker, he drops down below to see
The underside: mistakes, repairs, the costs,
The estimates, depreciated worth.

The headlights on the bridge illuminate
The road below. Time on his hands,
He counts the ways he saw the many men
Swindled from the promises they sought,

Then listens dumbfounded to evening's news
About the march across the bridge at Selma
That changed history, what they thought was true,
And what he thought was ever meant to be.

The horn sounds, bar lifts, traffic moves. He vows
The time has come to change his life and live.

The Player: His Crossing Pass
In Memory of Malcolm Livingston Goldie, 1895-1964

Each day, the shipyard horn announced the time
and changing shift. The children ran to find
their Grandfather, who walked up from the yard
on Commonwealth, and met them open-armed.

He worked at Quincy Shipyard for the war
And watched designs assembled on the floor
Balloon and blossom into finished drafts
Of battle. He fitted pipes and lined the shafts.

Destroyers, cruisers, warships, carriers
Were launched before the bridge where co-workers
All cheered as champagne cracked against the sides
That slid from berth to sea to meet the tides.

But that was part of his second career.
He came from Scotland decades earlier
To sign with the American Soccer League,
Who saw he had supply to meet demand,

How he moved to make the sweet assist
With ambidextrous skill, the crossing pass
That Archie Stark would pound into the goal.
Consistently, their parts defined the whole.

Each time he ran from far to middle ground,
He drew spectators just to see him play,
Then coached the college team at MIT,
Until an injured vertebrae, and he moved on.

From Clydebank, he arrived and made his name.
"One of the top wingers to play the game."
Pipe fitter, team player, asbestos in his lung.
He died at sixty-nine, a man still young.

The Salesman: The Gantry Crane

Engendering superlatives,
The strongest highest broadest crane
Defines the biggest job around,
Putting all the parts in place,

The housing for the longest ship,
The line and lift, the up and up,
Nothing to diminish by
Default but reach and swing on up.

And then the worst recession came.
Between the wars, the work was gone;
The contracts fell, the workers left
Or stayed, astride their Real Estate.

Each of these within the sight
Of hired crew and gantry crane.
Don't move it. Soon the times will change.
At least you have a standing frame.

The Pilot: Laws and Regulations

In sum, the tanker has the right of way.
A federal agency, the Coast Guard makes
Decisions that determine when the bridge
May open for the sake of the boat traffic.

The State Highway Department is the one
That will lift up the bridge, upon advance
Signals received from ships. The problem is
The tides, twelve hours apart, and the rush hour.

Tankers measuring five- to six-hundred
Feet depend on tides to clear the span.
It takes a tanker twenty minutes or
More to correct and change its forward course.

Need advance notice about the bridge?
Information for commuters can
Be sent through the Mass. Highway Department
Email. Fill in and sign the form below.

The Operator: Facts

The bridge goes up for at least fifteen minutes,
Or longer, five hundred and fifty times a year.
The wait can be twenty minutes, or so,
Is known to be, often, forty minutes.

Until Nineteen-eleven, the bridge was
An independent thing to operate.
The swing bridge could be opened by the hand
Of one man, or by man and boy alone.

But then, electric motors were installed,
One to lift, another on reserve.
As each structure wore out, it was replaced.
A tunnel underneath has been denied.

Walking across the bridge is discouraged.
I tell my kids, "Don't ever cross that bridge!"

The Provider: This Bridge Will Get You

Where water has no memory,
The bridge across it will remember.

In this, it is like our parents,
Reaching out, extended, tense,

Eager to show it wants to please
The ones it raised and flourished by,

Yet we walk all over it, steps
Clacking rudely, or wheels rumbling.

The span provides, laborious,
Alive with certainty, purpose.

It cannot fail to keep its grip
As it bears traffic over rivers'

Currents writhing with the pull
Of lunar influence and weathers.

We can be re-assured and know
That though the roads are stalled for miles,

This bridge remembers us, and at
The least, will get us on our way.

The Baker: Time to Rise

> *The soufflé was warm when carried across.*
> *It fell. We don't call it soufflé;*
> *We call it omelet. If made with fresh eggs,*
> *It never falls. Until it does.*
>
> *Steady with Cream of Tartar? Or yeast?*
> *Try without leavening? Baking powder,*
> *Baking soda, alone or together?*
> *My great aunt loved to add tapioca!*

The layer cake she brought across that day,
Baked on one side of the river to serve on the other,
Light as goose down, strong as a well-built house,
Was after the recipe learned from her mother.

When she arrived, the dining room table was set,
The steamers were ready to serve on the kitchen counter,
The chowder hot, the corn bread steaming. She
Put down the cake. Her family came in to join her.

They uncorked champagne and emptied the china plates.
The coffee was waiting; she cut through the heavenly cake.
It was airy as goose down, the icing sweet as a song.
The promise fulfilled, the timing was all.

It was a cake they remembered, a cake like no other,
Baked on one side of the bridge and the river, taken
Across a series of borders, natural, municipal,
All for the love of a son expressed by a mother.

How many borders had she crossed that day
For the sake of the cake that might have offended their taste?
Impediments loomed in her son's adventurous life
In another town with another impetuous wife.

But it turned out to be the cake they remembered, baked
And brought over the border, well-known and traveled and run,
Across the bridge and the river, all for the sake
Of the love borne by one woman for her son.

The Captain: Of the Seas

All up and down the coast, the land
Is joined by bridges like this one.
Limited by scope and time,
They soon fall short of nature's work,
Confusing dreams with amplitude.
I keep my bow turned toward the sea.

You cannot depend on a bridge
To mask the poorly charted course.
The journey is the searching for
The next good harbor, where you find
Temporary peace at anchor.
One can be free on the water.

The Minister: In Memoriam

The boy on the bicycle who had slipped beneath
The wheels of a car on the rain-slicked road surface
Would never join his father waiting up
For him, at home by the lamp in the window.

The woman who crept beneath the gate was not
Aware of the warning blast sent by the alarm,
Did not see the blinking lights as the floor rose up
And separated beneath her.

Ave Maria, pray for us, Mother of God.
We mourn the father's untimely loss of a son,
The sisters and daughters whose mother went out alone,
These unattended moments in time.

Ave Maria, pray for us, Mother of God.
Each sought to go forward and lost the way to get back.
They trusted, they stepped, they fell, and forfeited all.
The way up was down, the way forward stopped.

Pray for us, Mother of God. Ave Maria.

The Naturalist: River Gods

We underestimate the power of rivers:
Swollen, rushing, receding, and renewed,
Harnessed by commercial enterprise,

And when problems arise, we turn away.
What made us think the river would accept
This layering of planks? This flimsy bridge?

I came here looking for a life to live.
The river seemed a likely place to start,
A place to study man's and nature's art.

I built my dreams and aspirations here.
Now I find some dreams fulfilled, some flown,
A house paid for, children fully grown.

All that I have the river would dissolve.
Reflected in its surface sheen, I see
My need in old age, infancy, my face—

Frozen, then breaking; thawed, and then flowing again.
The river bears our trade and commerce on.
In spring, it proves to be a herring run.

The Celebrant: We Look Out Over the Water

Where fields once farmed
        And gathered up for fodder
Have been replaced
        By industry's upheavals,
Workhouse, warehouse,
        With each new project's ardor,
We look out for
        A glimpse, a changing color.
We look out over the water.

Below bridgegates,
        The out-sized foreign tanker
Maneuvers through
        And out into the harbor,
Where idle cranes,
        As if in patient slumber,
Keep arms aloft
        Not to be wrenched asunder.
We look out over the water.

We take these sights
        So achingly familiar
As traffic slows
        Each light a passing blinker
And count the days
        In winter, spring, and summer
That we can cross
        If someone holds the lever.
We look out over the water.

Big town, small city
    Common river border
We build one town
    And then we build the other.
Let us observe
    The time we spend together
And praise this bridge,
    Our most recent endeavor.
We look out over the water.

NOTES

Much of this poem was inspired by files of *The Patriot Ledger*, on microfilm beginning in 1837.

Timeline of the Bridge: timber pile 1800, swing bridge 1812, bascule 1934, vertical lift 1980s.

The Ferry, page 1
> Details from *The Quincy Patriot Ledger*, "History of Fore River Bridge Reflects Continuous Progress," August 4, 1934.

The Journalist, page 3
> From "New Bridge Is Unlikely before 2020." *The Boston Globe*, April 17, 2008.

The Optimist, page 5
> "…[M]y mind's eye tried to glimpse the future, and saw in a haze almost the same picture but with more smokestacks, more boats, and more geniality."— From "Morning at the Fore River: a Wayfarer's Impressionistic Sketch of Quincy's Industrial Harbor," *The Quincy Patriot Ledger*, August 17, 1925.

The Foreman, page 7
> Details from *The Quincy Patriot Ledger*: "Old Landmarks Give Way as New Bridge Rises Across Fore River," April 2, 1934, and "History of Fore River Bridge Reflects Continuous Progress," August 4, 1934.
> "The Hingham and Quincy Bridge and Turnpike Corporation was chartered 5th March, 1808, and opened for travel, with its two bridges over Fore and Back Rivers, connecting Quincy and Hingham, in 1812. These bridges, with their tolls from travelers and tolls to vessels passing through the draws, were a continual source of vexation and contention, which did not cease until the whole property was

thrown upon the towns as a public highway, 25th September 1862."
(www.weymouthhistoricalsociety.com)

The Lurker, page 11
U.S. Route 80 takes the Edmund Pettus Bridge in Selma, Alabama.

The Player, page 12
Malcolm Goldie biographical sketch from *American Soccer League* 1921 – 1931 by Colin Jose, The Scarecrow Press, Inc., Lanham, Maryland & London, 1998 (476-477).

The Salesman, page 13
Miller, Wayne G. *Fore River Shipyard.* Postcard History Series. Charleston: Arcadia Publishing. Copyright Wayne G. Miller, 2013.
Drummond, Dave. *The Shipyard. Will It Float?* Lincoln, NE: iUniverse, Inc. Copyright Dave Drummond, 2003.

The Pilot, page 14, and The Operator, page 15
"Bridge Control Out of States' Hands," *The Boston Globe*, February 2, 2006.

Joyce Wilson is editor of *The Poetry Porch*, which celebrated its twentieth anniversary online in May 2017. Wilson's poems have appeared in many literary journals, among them *American Arts Quarterly, Poetry Ireland, Ibbetson Street Magazine,* and *Alabama Literary Review.* Her full-length poetry collection, *The Etymology of Spruce,* and a chapbook, *The Springhouse,* both appeared in 2010. Her profiles of the poets Eavan Boland, Julia Budenz, and Etel Adnan can be read at the Women Poets Timeline Project at *Mezzo Cammin*. She directs a discussion group that welcomes all, the new-comers and the late-comers, to join in conversation about poetry once a month at the Scituate Town Library.

Taking classes as a special student at Harvard University for nearly a decade in the 1980s, Wilson received a B.A. through Harvard Extension in 1984 and a M.Ed. from the Graduate School of Education in 1987. During that time she studied writing poetry with Seamus Heaney, writing about poetry with Helen Vendler, in between seminars in English and American literature and education. She taught English at Boston University, and then Suffolk University, for almost two decades, during which time she often drove across the Fore River Bridge on her way to the Mass Transit stations in Quincy, Massachusetts, and on her way into Boston. During those years, she was caught on the drawbridge over the Fore River many times as it regulated traffic between the water ways and the road ways. She experienced the frustration of all varieties of commuters whose patience was tried by the need to wait for the floor of the bridge to rise and then fall again in order to get on with the start of their day, or to proceed on their way home at the end of the day.

Wilson and her husband have lived at the same address in Scituate, Massachusetts, for most of their adult lives. They continue to work on their acre of land, where they plant vegetables, tend to various perennial gardens, and raise flocks of chickens, who contribute their eggs and fertilizer to the ongoing process of growing things. They have travelled to Europe and the Middle East several times to catch up with their daughter, a journalist, now married with two daughters, who continues to cover the arts in Beirut, Lebanon, the locale of her great-grandparents.

www.ingramcontent.com/pod-product-compliance
Lightning Source LLC
LaVergne TN
LVHW041513070426
835507LV00012B/1545